No American has had a greater, or longer lasting, impact on law enforcement in America than John (J. Edgar) Hoover.

As head of the Federal Bureau of Investigation from 1924 (known then as the Bureau of Investigation), until his death in 1972, Director Hoover lead the battle against crime and corruption in the United States for nearly four decades and set the tone for the FBI's operation that still resonates through the halls of our Nation's premiere law enforcement agency.

His words, as published here, reflect his unique insight into the matters of crime, juvenile delinquency, the necessity of responsible parenting, community involvement and faith in the development of America's children.

Historical context and observations by author and Constitutional commentator Michael Scott provide the reader with perspective into the life of the Director, the times in which he lived and the aftermath of his life's work.

Works by Michael Scott Spillan

Writing as Michael Scott

Kelly's Fall

The Practice of Hypnosis and Hypnotherapy
2010 Edition, Editor and Contributor

Pillow Talk: A Comprehensive Guide to
Erotic Hypnosis & Relyfe Programming

Walking Papers: Title 28 U.S.C. §2255 Demystified
For Lawyers and Pro Se Litigants

The Science of the Mind in the Work of God:
A Primer on Ministerial Hypnosis & Hypnotherapy

ISBN-10:   0-9834164-5-1
ISBN-13:   9780-9834164-5-6

J. Edgar Hoover

on

Juvenile Delinquency

Blue Deck Press - Columbus, Ohio

J. Edgar Hoover on Juvenile Delinquency

On the tally sheet of accomplishments for youth in 1945, there are many marks that besmirch the record. The many fine attainments of American youngsters in their eager preparation to assume adult responsibilities have been smeared by the dishonest, antisocial behavior of boys and girls who seek happiness by illicit means.

There necessarily must be an answer to this problem of illegal, un-American behavior. An analysis of the structure of society inevitably includes a survey of man's attitudes and actions with relation to his fellow man. The progress of society depends upon man - its downfall is his responsibility. A nation's rise to great heights is based upon law and order. A nation's downfall, therefore, results from lawlessness and disorder.

Is it any wonder that right thinking Americans are anxious to preserve law and order to insure a continuance of free, democratic principles. The Nazi madmen plunged Europe into disorder. Their regime reaped a harvest of horror and death.

We should have great concern for our own home front because there is every indication that lawlessness and disorder are attempting to sink their fangs into our daily life. Crime is the offspring of these vicious evils and the records clearly indicate it is on the upswing.

J. Edgar Hoover on Juvenile Delinquency

A grand total of 1,565,541 major crimes were registered for our nation in 1945. This represented an increase of 12.4 percent over the 1944 figure. The crime increases were more pronounced and widespread in 1945 than have been recorded in many years. Sharp rises were noted in crimes of a serious nature. Robberies led with a 23.6 per cent jump followed by increases of 18.7 per cent in auto thefts, 17.0 per cent burglaries, 16.2 per cent in negligent manslaughters, and 10.1 per cent in murders. Aggravated assaults rose 8.7 per cent and an 8.6 per cent rise was recorded for larcenies. Offenses of rape, which for a number of years have been on the upswing, rose 5.7 per cent in 1945.

Crime with all its horror reaches its depths of despair in recounting the acts of boys and girls under 21 years of age. While only 21 per cent of the total number of persons arrested last year were youngsters under voting age, nevertheless they accounted for more than 40 per cent of the burglaries, 61 per cent of the car thieves, 30 per cent of the rapists, more than 22 per cent of the thieves and 35 per cent of the robbers arrested. The greatest increase in the arrest of boys was for criminal homicide and other assaults, such arrests increasing almost 17 per cent during 1945 compares with 1944. There was also a rise of almost 11 per cent of boys under 21 for offenses against common decency. The number of arrests of girls in the same age group for criminal homicide and other assaults showed a smaller upswing of 3 percent. Compared with 1941, arrests for females under 21 during 1945 increased more than 109 per cent.

There can be no doubt that juvenile delinquency persists as one of our most serious social problems. We can be secure in the conclusion that the problem is local and must be defeated in the community. It is obvious that the question of delinquency may differ in each community because of varying causative factors. Any approach to a solution of the question must first, I am certain, be a study of existing conditions which need to be remedied before an effective cure can take place.. If we begin to dispense some type of treatment before we know what kind of conditions need to be remedied, if the approach will, in all probability, be unsuccessful. In dealing with the personality and behavior of a delinquent, the community should get pertinent data which would yield the best picture as to why a youngster chose antisocial behavior, which in a majority of cases might ruin his chances for a healthy adulthood, over normal conduct.

Teen-age offenders, it is true, had the misfortune to grow up in a world unsettled by war. Our Country, during the past few years, was affected by a spirit of wartime abandon. Young people were left to shift for themselves, in all too many instances, as families became separated and homes broken. Community services and activities suffered a breakdown. Maladjustments in society influenced our youth to the end that juvenile delinquency increased tremendously during the war, and it has continued at a record level into the postwar period. The evidence is clear that we adults have been remiss in our duty to provide youth with an environment which will insure their development into decent, law abiding citizens.

More often than not, lack of parental care and guidance permeates the stories of the youngsters who have fallen into antisocial delinquency, in the majority of instances, arises from inherent evil tendencies on the part of children. Caught in the web of neglect, the youngsters are bitter examples of our failure as adults.

Parents who neglect to train their children in their fundamental obligations to society have violated the dignity of their parenthood and constitute a threat not only to their own family but to every man, woman and child in the community. I recall one case when an innocent, respectable citizen - the father of two young children - was murdered as the result of delinquency existing in other homes.

This man, his wife and children returned to their home one evening and noticed that the light was burning in their living-room radio. At that precise moment, noises were heard in the rear of the house. The husband went to the back part of the house to investigate and was shot and killed by two young hoodlums. Investigation revealed that two juveniles had entered the home through an unlocked back door and had tuned in the radio to the local police band so that they could be forewarned if a squad car was dispatched to the residence. The youths ransacked the house and stole miscellaneous jewelry, a child's bank and a .22 caliber rifle.

The two boys responsible for this dual crime were 12 and 15 years of age. The failure of their parents to train them as good citizens resulted in ruining their lives and imposed agonized grief on a law0abiding family. The twelve-year-old boy came from a home where discipline was unknown and the children were left to their own pursuits. The other lad came from a broken home where brutality had twisted and warped the minds of the children.

The problem of juvenile delinquency is not confined to any particular economic or social level. Like disease it strikes at homes of the poor and rich alike. Neither is the problem limited to any certain section of the country not the larger metropolitan areas. It exists any place where indifferent and self-centered parents, and short0sighted communities fail to discharge their obligations to the younger generation. A home which fails to reflect proper training, discipline, love, care and guidance is a source of infection and the children within are mentally starved.

In attaching the problem of juvenile crime, much emphasis mush be placed on the home. If the spiritual structure of the home is weak, decay will result to the nation. It is fundamental, therefore, that the moral stamina of our country depends upon our homes. In discussing the social importance of the home, it is necessary to recognize and understand the position of the family unit and the responsibilities of the parents in this bulwark of society. It is shockingly evident , when one reads case after case of youthful delinquency, that decay has hit the home and that parents have tossed their children upon the tempestuous waters of life unprepared to face the eddies and hidden shoals that lead to destruction.

It is difficult to realize why parents fail to shoulder the responsibilities for their parent-hood. Children who are forced into the back alleys of the community because a father or mother, or both are guilty of neglect, greed, selfishness, immorality or a score of other reasons, usually lack the moral fiber to offset temptation. I recall the case of Allen and Bill.

One winter evening while idly chatting to pass the leisure hours, Allen, age 17, confided in his 16-year old friend, Bill, that he was "broke" and would like to make some money. Burglary, they decided was the answer to their problem. They gained entrance into an electric service company in the neighborhood by forcing the rear basement door with a screw driver. Finding nothing of value in the office, the boys broke into the sale and removed several rolls of money. Before making their exit, at Bill's suggestion they set fire to the building since they had been unable to find anything of real value. Police picked up the youths before they had gone a block. The amount of loot was inconsequential, but the damage to the establishment by fire amounted to several thousand dollars. Both boys were armed at the time of the robbery.

Bill was turned over to the juvenile authorities. Because of his record, he was sent to the State Training School for an indefinite period. Allen was indicted by the Grand Jury on two charges of burglary and one charge of arson, and was sentenced to two years probation on each charge, the sentences to run concurrently and the first five months to be spent in the county jail.

Allen was the product of a broken home. His parents were divorced several years ago and his mother remarried shortly thereafter. Allen left home to live with his brother, his father and at various rooming houses. Although his mother asked him to reside with her, he resided in a hotel for two years and at the time of his arrest was living in a shabby rooming house. Allen admitted participating in four burglaries with Bill in addition to burglarizing a furniture store where he obtained a gun.

Bill resided with his parents until he was four years of age when he went to live with his grandparents. Upon his return home seven years later, his father had remarried and both parents had children by previous marriages to support. Bill's school records indicated that his deportment was fair, his scholastic record poor and that he had many unexplained tardinesses and absences. He had a sullen temper, was addicted to lying and stealing and frequently fought with his brothers and sisters.

Several years prior to the instant offense, Bill was placed on probation as a dependent child. Shortly after his discharge from probation, complaints were received regarding his immoral acts. He was committed to a parental school where he remained until shortly before the instant burglary. The boy admitted participation in four other burglaries.

I have related this case in some detail to show the evils incident to broken homes. If we seek an effective remedy for the problem of youthful crime, we must strengthen the spiritual structure of our homes. Parents as the child's first teacher, must dispense along with love and affection, an overflowing measure of moral teaching and ethical values. We gamble away the future of America if we fail to instill in the hearts and minds of every child the necessity of placing the interests of the family and the nation above his own.

May I urge parents in America to give good example to their youngsters by their actions, attitudes and words. The mind of a child will receive impressions with ease. If these impressions are good, they will form the basis for the ideals that will strengthen adulthood.

The saying, "Train up a child in the way he should go: and when he is old he will not depart from it," is as true today as it was thousands of years ago when it was written.

In the training of children, it would appear that there is a tendency to discount or eliminate the teachings of God. In their eagerness to prepare their children for the material things of the world, many parents miss the most important thing - religion. The failure to instill in youngsters the necessity to follow established moral and ethical teachings places their future security and ours in jeopardy. Their minds are void of reason as to why it is necessary to follow the moral and man-made law. Their consciences will be warped and scarred and their will power will be exercised to satisfy their own selfish ends. The terrible consequence of that type of make-up is usually vicious criminal activity.

The awful gash which has cut into the surface of our society as a result of crime needs to be cured by a return to fundamentals and an abiding fath in God. No one can successfully substitute for parents in teaching a child the beauties of liberty and freedom as distinguished from license and anarchy. The lessons a child learns from his parents are absorbed with trust and implicit faith. That is why there can be no suitable substitute for parents; no adequate substitute for their home.

J. Edgar Hoover on Juvenile Delinquency

Failure on the part of parents has made it necessary for our churches, schools and youth-serving organizations to do all they can try to retrieve youngsters from the results of bad example. These agencies in our social structure are doing fine work to create solidarity on the youth front.

There are many distracting factors that influence the actions of youth in modern life. It is increasingly evident that all of us must contribute our thought, time and effort to the solution of a problem which presents a grave threat to our American way of life.

A study of the individual backgrounds of many youthful offenders reveals a complete lack of opportunity for proper recreation and worthwhile leisure-time activity. During the way, the facilities of nearly every community swung into action toward a common objective. Youth was left, for the most part, on its own and little was done to create wholesome opportunities for diversion and provide proper outlets for normal, youthful vigor. We cannot discount the fact youths have the desire to do something. This desire cannot be misguided or uncontrolled or it will lead to ruin. Work, play and the utilization of youthful ambitions can be properly coordinated and directed. If a community is blessed with that type of activity, it is bound to give America healthy, morally clean boys and girls who are ready and eager to inherit the responsibilities of adulthood.

J. Edgar Hoover on Juvenile Delinquency

We of law enforcement welcome the assistance of civic-minded Americans who are generously striving to prevent crime. Fundamentally, it is the job of law enforcement to apprehend criminals. We are also anxious to prevent crime. Our task is hopeless, however, unless every American is willing to help made available for our youth worthwhile pursuits and leisure-time activities. It is of paramount importance that adult America not be charged with setting a bad example for youngsters.

The problem of delinquency in your community may differ in degree and kind from other communities. I strongly urge you to support any worth-while project which attempts to analyze the problem in your locality. Encourage and assist the youth-serving organizations which are, with success, devoting their efforts to channelizing youthful activity along constructive lines. Actively assist your church in its work for youth. The influence of the church is wide-sweeping. Its contribution toward society and its power for good are unlimited.

Decent, right-thinking Americans have every right to wish for a continuation of the principles that made this country great. All of us want a vigorous, healthy nation where the laws of justice and equity firmly prevail. We must firmly resolve now to enter the battle against crime and other vicious influences which tend to infect our youth and destroy their chances of becoming true Americans.

J. Edgar Hoover on Juvenile Delinquency

We cannot wait for tomorrow in seeking to improve the lot of youth. We must begin today.

_____

In 1895, America was still recovering from the throws of civil war. Three decades had not yet served to heal the wounds of the most destructive war in U.S. history. Immigrants were pouring into the country from all around the world seeking dreams of freedom and opportunity, sometimes finding industrial nightmare while working 18 hours days, but more often finding success in the increasingly diverse communities of the New World.

Just six years after the last of the Indian wars, and less than a year after his birth in an immigrant dominated section of Washington, D.C., the world John Edgar Hoover was born into would find the Supreme Court upholding the "separate but equal" Jim Crow laws cementing the next 70 years tumultuous race relations.

America, at the turn of the Twentieth Century, was a place of fantastic growth and dramatic contradiction. The future director of the FBI was 25 years old before the right to vote was guaranteed to American women in 1920 and nationalistic pride was not so great that internal prejudices would not be strong enough to set Italians against Irish against Germans against everyone[1].

Like America, J. Edgar Hoover was a study in contradiction. A warrior for the protection of the American way of life, his means seem contrary to his purposes.

For instance, being a powerful leader in federal law enforcement, Hoover, himself of German ancestry,

---

[1]It is interesting to note that it was during this post - Civil War era that we Americans, and people around the world, first started thinking about the United States as being truly one nation, as opposed to a collection of independent states operating under more of an imperial model. This change is most evident when reading news from around the world. Prior to the war references would almost universally read things like "the United States announced today that they are....." or just "the United States are..." indicating by their language that the country was in fact a collections of states. In the years after the war, it became common to see "..the United States is..." or "the United States announced today that it would..." Showing that we, and in fact the peoples of the world, saw a true nation as opposed to a federation of separate governments, separate peoples.

led the push for surveillance of German Americans in the decade leading up to the second World War.

A forceful lecturer on the subject of American liberties, Hoover, twice sworn to protect the Constitution (first as a lawyer and then as Director of a Justice Department agency), pushed President Truman hard to suspend *habeas corpus* and allow him to arrest 12,000 Americans he decided *may be disloyal* at the beginning of the Korean War and was repeated frustrated by the actions of the Supreme Court in assuring the civil rights of individuals over the arbitrary actions sometimes over zealous FBI and local law enforcement agents.

Rumors and innuendo abound regarding the reasons for J. Edgar's driven nature (Truman Capote took such glee in spreading salacious rumors about the Director that he once famously remarked that he was more interested in upsetting Hoover than he was in determining whether the rumors were true), though none of those rumors ever proved out, and while the FBI of the time often trampled on both the Constitution and the rights of Americans, the Director's very real contributions to justice and to protecting our national way of life cannot be understated.

J. Edgar Hoover on Juvenile Delinquency

The FBI crime labs, prevention of several very real communist plots and illegal activities, the Quirin affair, the Verona Project and so many other countless accomplishments cannot be discounted. To be honest, the man was a machine, a zealot for the protection of the nation he loved (as he saw it). He, in his obsession (often tempered, of necessity, by calmer minds), protected the United States for over four decades and we, the beneficiaries of that protection, undeniably owe a debt of gratitude to the man and his zeal.

The Author:

J. Edgar Hoover held the position of FBI Director longer than any other person, over four decades.

In 1946 he wrote the words contained in this work in the hopes of inspiring others to become involved with the young people in their communities and that it might, in some small way, curb the advancing tide of juvenile delinquency in the United States.

Director Hoover has been one of the most controversial government leaders in U.S. History and was, without a doubt, been the one with the greatest impact on American law enforcement.

John Hoover died in 1972, at the age of 77. At the time of his death he had been director of the FBI for 42 years.

The Commentator:

Michael Scott is the pen name of a prolific author on the subject of Constitutional rights. A federal inmate in the 1990's, Mr. Scott won the liberty of fellow inmates through several court actions and, upon his release became a successful writer of federal sentencing memorandums, direct appeals and post-conviction challenges, working for *pro se* litigants and attorneys around the mid-west.

In recent years Mr. Scott, working with others, developed the Relyfe Programming approach to hypnosis and hypnotherapy and has published three books and several articles on the use of hypnosis in the healing process.

For more information about Blue Deck Press publications visit: www.BlueDeckPress.com

For information on Mr. Scott's work in hypnosis visit: www.Relyfe-Online.com